USING THE
SCIENTIFIC
METHOD

Kirsten W. Larson

Rourke
Educational Media

rourkeeducationalmedia.com

Scan for Related Titles
and Teacher Resources

Before Reading:

Building Academic Vocabulary and Background Knowledge

Before reading a book, it is important to tap into what your child or students already know about the topic. This will help them develop their vocabulary, increase their reading comprehension, and make connections across the curriculum.

1. *Look at the cover of the book. What will this book be about?*
2. *What do you already know about the topic?*
3. *Let's study the Table of Contents. What will you learn about in the book's chapters?*
4. *What would you like to learn about this topic? Do you think you might learn about it from this book? Why or why not?*
5. *Use a reading journal to write about your knowledge of this topic. Record what you already know about the topic and what you hope to learn about the topic.*
6. *Read the book.*
7. *In your reading journal, record what you learned about the topic and your response to the book.*
8. *After reading the book complete the activities below.*

Content Area Vocabulary
Read the list. What do these words mean?

analyze
communicate
compare
control
dependent variable
discrepancy
impact
inconclusive
independent variable
interpreted
manipulates
nocturnal
observe
peer
process
reasoning
rigorous
techniques
variable

After Reading:

Comprehension and Extension Activity

After reading the book, work on the following questions with your child or students in order to check their level of reading comprehension and content mastery.

1. *Who can we credit the discovery of the scientific method to? (Summarize)*
2. *Who uses the information generated by scientists? (Asking questions)*
3. *Look around the room. What kind of questions would you test? (Text to self connection)*
4. *Explain what discrepancy means. (Summarize)*
5. *Why is evidence so important to scientists? (Asking questions)*

Extension Activity

Make the connection and think like a scientist! Using the scientific method, construct the best recipe for bubbles using dish soap and water. What different brands of dish soap will you use? How much water and dish soap will be necessary to create the best bubble recipe? What is your variable in this experiment? Follow the scientific method by creating a hypothesis, procedure, recording your data, and analyzing your results.

TABLE OF CONTENTS

CHAPTER ONE

SCIENCE STEP BY STEP

In 1919, Canadian Dr. Frederick Banting read about the pancreas in a medical journal. His reading gave him an idea. Could he suck insulin out of the pancreas and use it to treat people with diabetes?

Banting designed an experiment, a scientific test. He tied off part of the pancreas in a few dogs and drew out insulin. This chemical unlocks your cells letting blood sugar inside. In other dogs, he removed the pancreas to cause diabetes.

Banting gave insulin shots to the sick dogs. After many tries, he found out his guess was right. Giving insulin lowered the dogs' blood sugar!

Student Charles Best (left) helped Dr. Charles Banting (right) with his research. Here, the two stand with one of the diabetic dogs used in the trials.

How the Pancreas Works

Stomach turns
food into glucose

Glucose enters
the bloodstream

Pancreas
releases insulin

Insulin allows glucose
to enter cells throughout
the body

The shots worked in people too! Banting published his results in a medical journal to share his discovery with other scientists.

People with diabetes give themselves injections to maintain proper blood sugar levels.

All scientists must follow the scientific method when conducting experiments.

Banting used a **process** called the scientific method to make his discovery. The scientific method is a step-by-step process for solving science problems. Scientists use it every day.

The Scientific Method

OBSERVE
and ask questions.

RESEARCH

Make a
HYPOTHESIS

Design and conduct an
EXPERIMENT

ANALYZE
results, draw conclusions,
and share them.

The scientific method has five parts. First, look around and ask questions. Then, research to find out what scientists already know about the problem. Make a guess, called a hypothesis. Test that guess. Finally, **analyze** results, **develop** a conclusion, and share what you learned.

Sounds easy. But sometimes the scientific method isn't so straightforward. Often, scientists move back and forth between the steps. After some experiments, they may revise their guess. Or they may have to change parts of the experiment.

Banting had to change his experiment when a patient was allergic to insulin. Banting purified the insulin more and redid the test.

CHAPTER TWO

REAL WORLD, REAL SCIENCE

You probably use parts of the scientific method already. During track practice, you notice a friend's high-tech shirt seems dry, but your cotton shirt is soaked. What's going on?

Why do high-tech shirts dry quicker than cotton?

Guess what? You've just checked off the first step of the scientific method: observing and asking questions. When you **observe**, you study something carefully. When you really pay attention, you may see some patterns. After checking out all your classmates' shirts, you wonder, do manmade fabrics dry faster?

You have the makings of a science experiment. You can test how fast different shirts dry. But here's the thing. In science, you can't just ask any question. It has to be one you can test.

Try testing this question: Which shirt looks the best? You and your classmates probably have different opinions. There's no one answer.

Questions about opinions cannot be answered using the scientific method.

Research is an essential step when investigating a scientific question.

Now you're ready for research, which is the second step. Research helps you form a temporary answer to your question. It might give you clues about designing your test. Check out books from the library and scan the Internet for recent information.

Make sure that your hypothesis is written in the form of a statement, not a question.

In the third step of the method, you answer your question with an educated guess called a hypothesis. This guess often takes the form of an "if..., then..." statement. Your hypothesis could be: If a shirt is made of manmade fabric, then it will dry faster.

The hypothesis tries to relate two things. In this case, you are testing the relationship between the fabric and how fast shirts dry.

Manmade Fabric

Cotton Fabric

Variable A	Size	Color	Water	Variable B
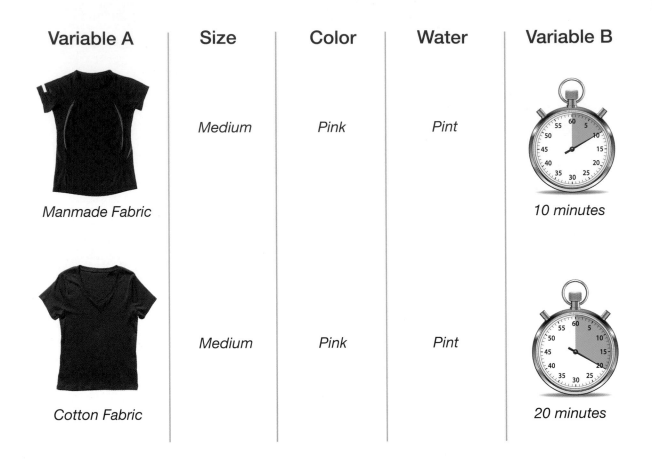 Manmade Fabric	Medium	Pink	Pint	10 minutes
Cotton Fabric	Medium	Pink	Pint	20 minutes

Many scientists test their guess through a controlled test called an experiment, which is the fourth step. This helps them understand how changing one thing affects something else. Anything that changes in an experiment is called a **variable**. Variables vary, or change.

For your shirt experiment, you change the shirts' fabric. That's one variable. So is the drying time. Everything else, like shirt size, color, the amount of water, and time spent in the dryer should be the same. Otherwise, you wouldn't know if the fabric or the shirt size changed the drying time.

Vexing Variables

*Variables can be vexing. But they don't have to be. Scientists work with two main types. The **independent variable** is what the scientist controls. In your experiment, you conduct tests with different kinds of fabric. The fabric is the part that you change. It is the independent variable.*

*When you change the fabric, other changes occur. That change is the drying time. Drying time is the change that your experiment is designed to measure. The change you measure is the **dependent variable**.*

The dependent variable depends on the independent variable. There would be no change in drying time if there were not different fabrics to compare. In this way, dependent and independent variables work together in an experiment.

Independent Variable

Dependent Variable

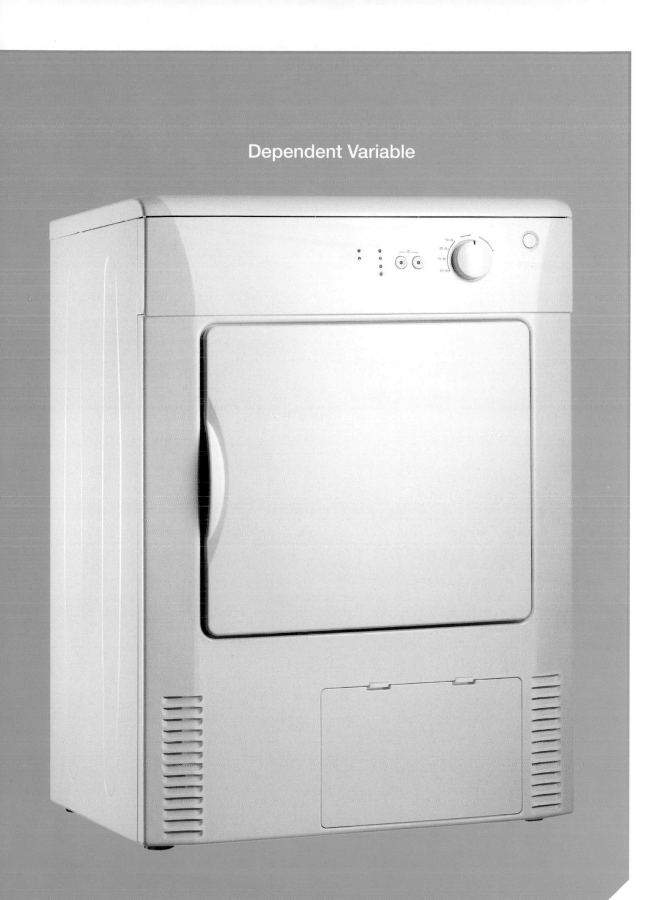

To make sure they do everything the same, scientists write down the steps they will follow, called a procedure. Think of it like a recipe for the experiment. When it's time to do the experiment, they run it many times.

Procedure

Equipment: Cotton shirt, high-tech shirt, 2 buckets, measuring cup, dryer, timer, tap water, thermometer

Procedure:
1) Pour one pint of cool water into a bucket. Water should be 60 degrees.
2) Place shirt in bucket.
3) Set timer for 10 minutes.
4) Place shirt in dryer.
5) Set dryer for 30 minutes, but check shirt every 5 minutes until dry.
6) Note shirt type and drying time in science notebook.
7) Repeat with other shirt.

Test 1

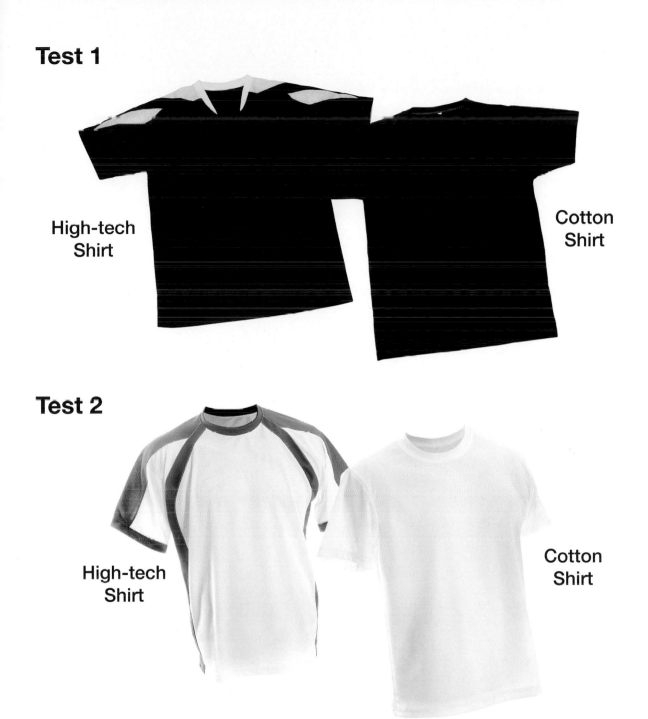

High-tech
Shirt

Cotton
Shirt

Test 2

High-tech
Shirt

Cotton
Shirt

In your test, you might use a black cotton and a black high-tech shirt. for the first test. In the second round, you pick white shirts of the same two materials. You take measurements of how dry the shirts feel every five minutes. You keep a record of your results. The evidence, or information, will prove if your guess was right.

Staying in control

*Many lab experiments use a **control** group to allow scientists to compare results. In medical studies, one group of patients takes a new drug. A control group takes a pill that looks like the drug. But this pill contains no medicine. If the group taking the new drug gets better, while the control group doesn't, scientists know the new medicine worked.*

Before they arrive at their conclusion, scientists have to analyze their evidence. They often use graphs to help them see the big picture.

When you make a graph of fabric and average drying times, you see the high-tech fabrics win every time. You conclude that your hypothesis was correct.

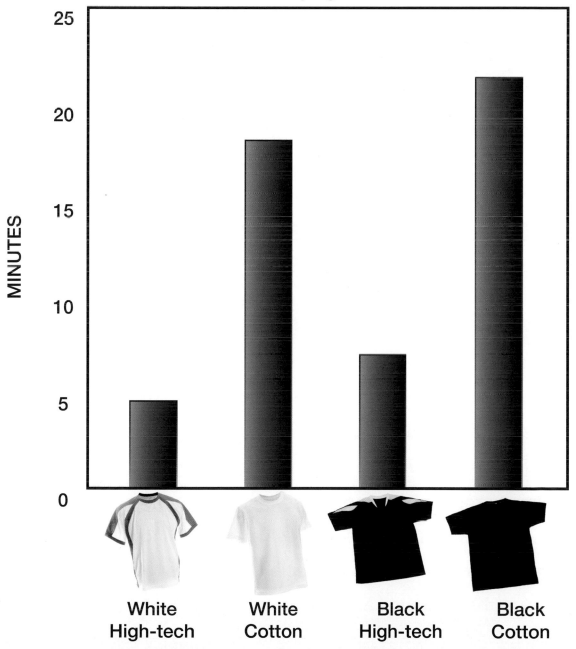

Drying Time

Other scientists copy an experiment to make sure the results are accurate.

Scientists share their results widely so other scientists can review and challenge them. One way scientists **communicate** is by publishing reports in journals.

Before a journal will print a report, the editor asks other scientists to review it. This process is called **peer** review. Reviewers look at the procedure, evidence, and how that evidence was **interpreted**. A second way scientists share results is by presenting their findings at scientific meetings.

Scientists share their findings with experts in their field.

CHAPTER THREE

MAKINGS OF THE METHOD

The scientific method is fairly new. Early people used stories, called **myths**, to explain how the world worked. The ancient Greeks thought thunder and lightning were weapons of the god Zeus. Ancient Egyptians thought the god Set made lightning with his spear. Each group had their own explanations for things.

Today, we know that lightning is caused by an electric discharge in the clouds.

In ancient Greece, philosophers Plato and Aristotle used logic and reason to explain the world.

About 2,500 years ago, things started to change. In Greece, people like Aristotle used some **techniques** that became part of the scientific method. They observed nature, asked questions about what they saw, and made guesses.

However, instead of experimenting, people like Aristotle used **reason** to explain what they saw. For example, Aristotle thought the Earth was the center of the universe. It sure looks like it from our point of view, and Aristotle talked about all the reasons his idea could be true. But Aristotle never tested his guess. Although he was wrong, Aristotle and other people of his time had shifted to a more scientific way of thinking.

Aristotle's Universe

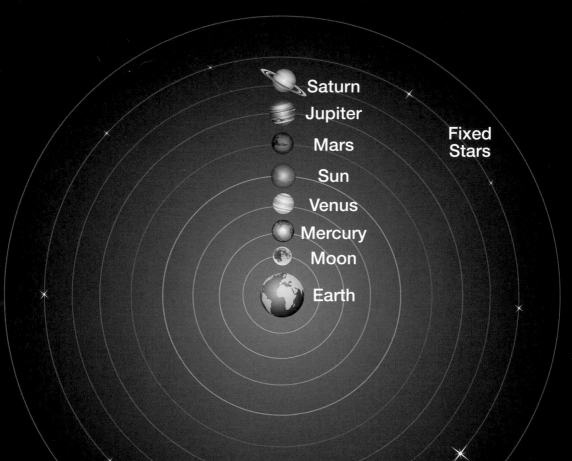

Aristotle believed that Earth was at the center of the universe. He identified seven "wandering stars": the Moon, Mercury, Venus, the Sun, Mars, Jupiter, and Saturn. The rest of the stars in the sky were "fixed stars."

Galileo Puts Aristotle to the Test

Italian astronomer and physicist Galileo Galilei was one of the first to challenge some of Aristotle's reasoning. Aristotle reasoned that heavier things fell faster. Galileo tested this idea by rolling balls down ramps. He used water clocks to measure how they sped up. Galileo's experiments proved that things speed up at the same rate regardless of their size.

By the 1600s, the scientific method began to take shape thanks to Sir Francis Bacon. An English scientist and politician, Bacon urged his peers to observe, make a guess, experiment, and share results. He published his ideas in a book called the *Novum Organum*. Bacon's views paved the way for the process scientists use today.

Sir Frances Bacon (1561–1626)

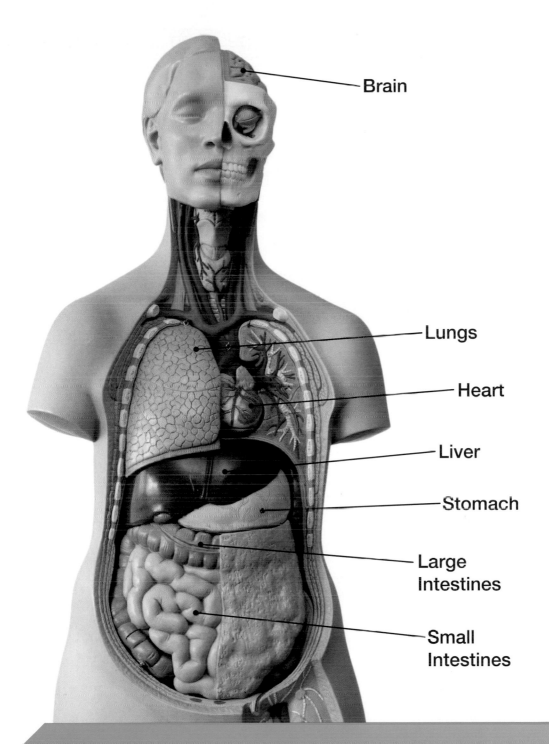

Brain

Lungs

Heart

Liver

Stomach

Large
Intestines

Small
Intestines

See for Yourself

*For centuries, people thought the body was made of four things:
blood, phlegm, yellow bile, and black bile. In the 1500s, Belgian doctor
Andreas Vesalius decided to test these ideas. He dissected human bodies
so he could peek inside. Vesalius learned that this theory was wrong.*

Scientists collect evidence through observations.

Today, scientists can't just make up stories about how things work. They have to collect evidence to back up their claims. The scientific method helps weed out wrong ideas through **rigorous** testing and peer review. It means only the best ideas are accepted over time.

This is important because scientific ideas have the power to change the way we think about the world around us. Powerful people like politicians may look to science when passing laws. Doctors use science to heal people.

Politicians and business leaders take scientific evidence into account when making important decisions.

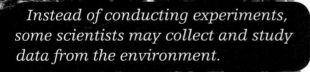

Instead of conducting experiments, some scientists may collect and study data from the environment.

Even though most scientists rely on the scientific method, they use it in different ways. Some do lab experiments. Others gather evidence in the field. Let's meet some real, live scientists and explore the scientific method at work.

CHAPTER FOUR

SCIENTIFIC METHOD IN ACTION

Dr. Zia Nisani pokes and prods a scorpion in a beaker. The scorpion whips its tail and strikes, releasing its venom. Zing! Nisani catches the liquid so he can study it. This was all part of his plan.

Scorpions release venom though their sharp stingers.

Rattlesnakes release more venom when attacking larger prey. Would scorpions do the same?

Nisani uses the scientific method in his lab to study animal behavior. Nisani wondered how much venom scorpions release in different situations. Do scorpions inject more venom when they feel threatened? His question came from a study that he read about rattlesnakes. Their bites pack more venom when their prey is bigger.

Nisani gathered research. He found that spiders also **control** how much venom they release. Nisani guessed that scorpions would have a similar behavior. His hypothesis was: If making venom takes a lot of energy, then scorpions will release more only when they feel more threatened.

With hypothesis in hand, Nisani carefully designed his experiment. He made sure the experiment would be safe for himself and for the scorpions. Since he wanted to know how scorpions dole out their venom, a key variable was the amount of venom they release with each sting. He would measure the liquid's volume.

Scientists use special tools to measure liquid volume. The small amounts of venom a scorpion releases are measured in microliters using a very small syringe.

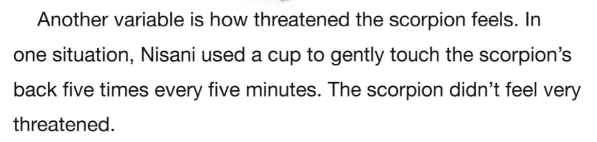

Scientists take precautions to make sure that they are unharmed by animals during experiments.

Another variable is how threatened the scorpion feels. In one situation, Nisani used a cup to gently touch the scorpion's back five times every five minutes. The scorpion didn't feel very threatened.

In another situation, he poked the scorpion every five seconds. It felt under attack. How threatened the scorpion feels is Nisani's **independent variable**. It's the piece that he **manipulates** in the lab so he can measure the amount of venom, which is the **dependent variable**.

39

Except for the independent variable, Nisani kept everything else the same. He used the same type of cup to prod them. They lived in the same type of sandy habitat. They ate one cricket every week. If Nisani changed any one of these things, he wouldn't know what **affected** the volume of venom.

Many scorpions live in sandy, desert habitats.

Then it was time to get the scorpions stinging. Nisani tested six scorpions so he could see a general pattern. Then he did the whole experiment again in a second trial, or run through. This gave him enough information to draw conclusions.

Nisani used mathematical analysis and graphs to see his results. Graphs let him easily **compare** how much venom the scorpions released with each sting. As he suspected, the scorpions injected more venom when they were more threatened.

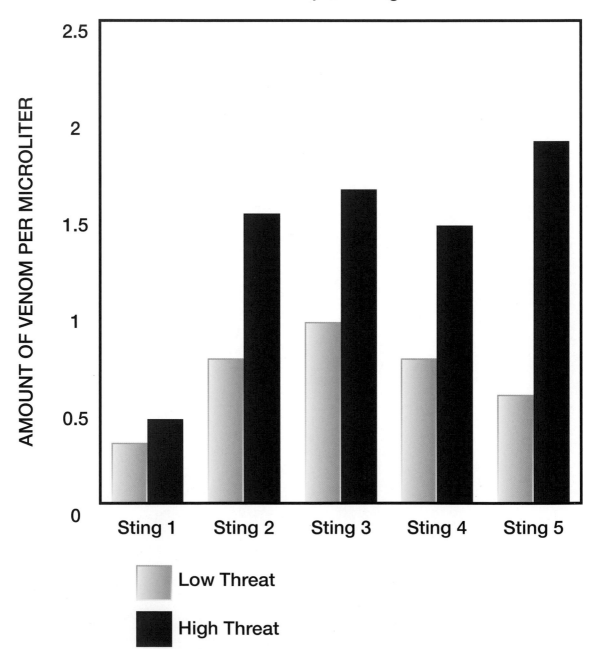

Data Discrepancies

*Using graphs and math shows scientists when data doesn't quite fit the pattern. In a different experiment, Nisani noticed one piece of information was very different from the rest. What caused the **discrepancy**?*

*Someone had switched on the light in the scorpions' room. Scorpions are **nocturnal**, and Nisani's procedure called for them to be in the dark for a full 12 hours. This blast of light could have caused the difference in his data. Because he knew the source of the error, Nisani didn't use the tests from the scorpions that had been exposed to light.*

Before he could share his conclusion, Nisani questioned his process. Did he test both female and male scorpions? Old and young? If he did, then he can make some general conclusions about scorpion venom. If he only used female scorpions, for example, his data would be **inconclusive**. Maybe female scorpions control how much venom they release, but not males.

Confident of his results, Nisani wrote up his paper so he could share his discovery.

Scientists never stop asking why, even when they are in the middle of an experiment. During a **recent** test, Nisani noticed a scorpion waving a hairy pincer up and down when a predator was near. He wonders if scorpions use those hairs like insects use their antennae. He's planning an experiment to find out.

In science, the end of the scientific method is not really the end at all. It's just a new beginning.

GLOSSARY

analyze (AN-uh-lize): to study something carefully to make sense of it

communicate (kuh-MYOO-ni-kate): to share information about something

compare (kuhm-PAIR): to judge the similarities and differences among multiple things

control (kuhn-TROL): in an experiment, something you use as a comparison

dependent variable (di-PEN-duhnt VAIR-ee-uh-buhl): what is measured in an experiment; the part of the experiment that may change

discrepancy (dis-KREP-uhn-see): something that is different from what it should be

impact (IM-pakt): a major effect

inconclusive (in-kuhn-KLOO-siv): data that is unclear or uncertain

independent variable (in-di-PEN-duhnt VAIR-ee-uh-buhl): the variable that you have control of and purposefully change during an experiment

interpreted (in-TUR-prit-ed): decided what something means

manipulates (muh-NIP-yuh-lates): to control something skillfully

nocturnal (nahk-TUR-nuhl): an animal that is active at night

observe (uhb-ZURV): to watch something closely

peer (peer): someone with the same age, rank, or area of knowledge

process (PRAH-ses): a series of actions in a procedure

reasoning (REE-zuhn-een): logical thinking

rigorous (rig-UR-uhs): very strict and demanding

techniques (tek-NEEKS): a method of doing something that requires skill

variable (VAIR-ee-uh-buhl): in science, something that changes

46

INDEX

WEBSITES TO VISIT

http://www.sciencebuddies.org/science-fair-projects/project_scientific_
method.shtml

http://www.nasa.gov/audience/foreducators/plantgrowth/reference/
Scientific_Method.html#.UsYFdGRDs40

http://www.brainpop.com/educators/community/bp-jr-topic/scientific-
method/

ABOUT THE AUTHOR

Kirsten W. Larson spent six years at NASA before writing for young people. She's met Curiosity's twin, the test rover, and worked with NASA's DC-8 crews during science missions. Her articles appear in ASK, ODYSSEY, AppleSeeds, and Boys' Quest. She lives with her husband and two sons near Los Angeles, California.

Meet The Author!
www.meetREMauthors.com

© 2015 Rourke Educational Media

www.rourkeeducationalmedia.com

PHOTO CREDITS: Cover and Title Page © Chepko Danill Vitalevich; page 4 © AP Images; page 5 © Alex Luengo; page 6 © Image Point fr; page 7 © michaeljung; page 8 © Kimberlywood; page 9 © Alexander Raths; page 10, 11 © Steve Debenport; page 12 © Ruslan Dashinsky; page 13 © sturti; page 14, 22, 32 © Wavebreak Media Ltd; page 15, 16, 18 © Dominik Pabis, mirofanova; page 17 © juffin, keenon; page 19 © ilkay muratoglu; page 20 © mongkoi chakritthakool; page 21, 23 © Heavenman, Yuttask Jannarong; InGreen; page 24 © zhudifeng; page 25 © vgajic; page 26 © mikexpert; 28 © vectomart; page 29 © timurock, CTE Consulting Services; page 30 wikipedia.com; page 31 © arcady31; page 33 © heroimages; page 34 © goodluz; page 35 © EcoPrint; page 36 © Audrey Snider-Bell; page 37 © Cathy Keifer; page 39 © Danny Smythe, 2happy; page 40 © EcoPrint; page 41 © sebastianPuda; page 43 © Alberto Romares; page 45 © Rossette Jordaan

Edited by: Jill Sherman

Cover and Interior design by: Tara Raymo

Library of Congress PCN Data

Using the Scientific Method / Kirsten W. Larson
(Let's Explore Science)
ISBN 978-1-62717-748-1 (hard cover)
ISBN 978-1-62717-870-9 (soft cover)
ISBN 978-1-62717-980-5 (e-Book)
Library of Congress Control Number: 2014935673

Also Available as:

ROURKE'S
e-Books